SNAKE BITE

Tom Jackson

🌳 Crabtree Publishing Company

www.crabtreebooks.com

Crabtree Publishing Company

www.crabtreebooks.com   1-800-387-7650

**Published
in Canada
Crabtree Publishing**
616 Welland Ave.
St. Catharines, ON
L2M 5V6

**Published in the
United States
Crabtree Publishing**
PMB16A
350 Fifth Ave., Suite 3308
New York, NY 10118

Content development by Shakespeare Squared
www.ShakespeareSquared.com
First published in Great Britain in 2008 by ticktock Media Ltd,
2 Orchard Business Centre, North Farm Road,
Tunbridge Wells, Kent, TN2 3XF
Copyright © ticktock Entertainment Ltd 2008

Author: Tom Jackson
Project editor: Ruth Owen
Project designer: Sara Greasley
Photo research: Lizzie Knowles
Proofreaders: Crystal Sikkens,
  Robert Walker
Production coordinator:
  Katherine Kantor
Prepress technicians:
  Katherine Kantor, Ken Wright

With thanks to series
editors Honor Head
and Jean Coppendale,
and consultant
Sally Morgan.

Thank you to Lorraine
Petersen and the
members of nasen

Picture credits:
Alamy: Jeff Greenberg: p. 28
Corbis: How Hwee Young/epa: p. 11; Jeffrey L. Rotman:
  p. 25; Rungroj Yongrit/epa: p. 13
FLPA: p. 16–17; Michael & Patricia Fogden/Minden
  Pictures: p. 7, 21, 29; Claus Meyer/ Minden Pictures: p. 6
Naturepl.com: Bruce Davidson: p. 12; Tony Phelps:
  p. 29 (bottom); Michael Richards/John Downer: p. 8
NHPA: Daniel Heuclin: p. 4, 24; Bill Love: p. 15
Photolibrary Group: p. 26
Shutterstock: cover, p. 1, 2, 5, 9, 14, 18, 19, 20, 22–23, 31
SuperStock: age fotostock: p. 10

Every effort has been made to trace copyright holders, and we apologize in
advance for any omissions. We would be pleased to insert the appropriate
acknowledgments in any subsequent edition of this publication.

Library and Archives Canada Cataloguing in Publication

Jackson, Tom, 1972-
    Snake bite / Tom Jackson.

(Crabtree contact)
Includes index.
ISBN 978-0-7787-3772-8 (bound).--ISBN 978-0-7787-3794-0 (pbk)

    1. Poisonous snakes--Juvenile literature. 2. Snakebites--
Juvenile literature. I. Title. II. Series.

QL666.O6J32 2008   j597.96'165   C2008-905957-3

Library of Congress Cataloging-in-Publication Data

Jackson, Tom, 1972-
  Snake bite / Tom Jackson.
      p. cm. -- (Crabtree contact)
  Includes index.
  ISBN-13: 978-0-7787-3794-0 (pbk. : alk. paper)
  ISBN-10: 0-7787-3794-2 (pbk. : alk. paper)
  ISBN-13: 978-0-7787-3772-8 (reinforced library binding : alk. paper)
  ISBN-10: 0-7787-3772-1 (reinforced library binding : alk. paper)
  1. Poisonous snakes--Juvenile literature. 2. Snakebites--Juvenile
literature. I. Title. II. Series.

QL666.O6J26 2009
597.96--dc22
                                                   2008039395

CONTENTS

KILLER SNAKES

Every year, 100,000 people die from snake bites! Most **victims** live in the countrysides of Africa, India, and Southeast Asia.

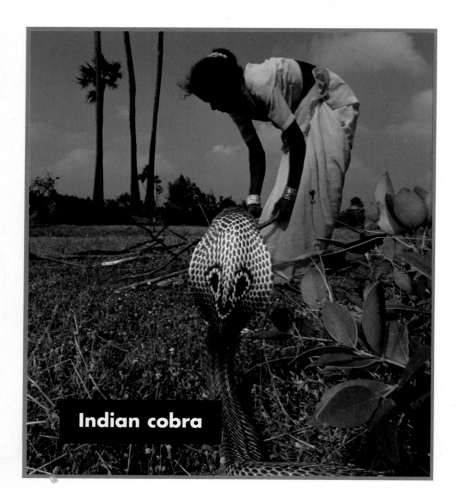

Indian cobra

People die from snake bites because they cannot get to a hospital for treatment. The **venom** in the snake bites attack their bodies before they can get medical help.

Cape cobra

The Cape cobra is one of Africa's most dangerous snakes. The venom in a single bite can kill a person in just a few hours.

FANGS

Close-up of a snake's mouth

Fang

Drop of venom

Snake venom is poisonous saliva.

Snakes bite their **prey**
with two long, pointed
teeth called **fangs**.

The squirt venom through
the fangs.

Hog-nosed
pit viper

Fangs

Frog

The snake's venom
goes straight into
its prey's blood.

VENOM

There are two main types of snake venom.

Neurotoxin

How it works: A neurotoxin stops **nerves** and muscles from working. The nerves cannot carry messages from the brain to the muscles in the body.
What happens: The victim cannot breathe. It also stops the heart from working. Without treatment, the victim will die within hours.
Snakes with this venom: cobras, mambas

Spitting cobra

Spitting cobras spray their venom into the eyes of **predators** to blind the animals. They can hit their target from more than 9 feet (2.7 meters) away!

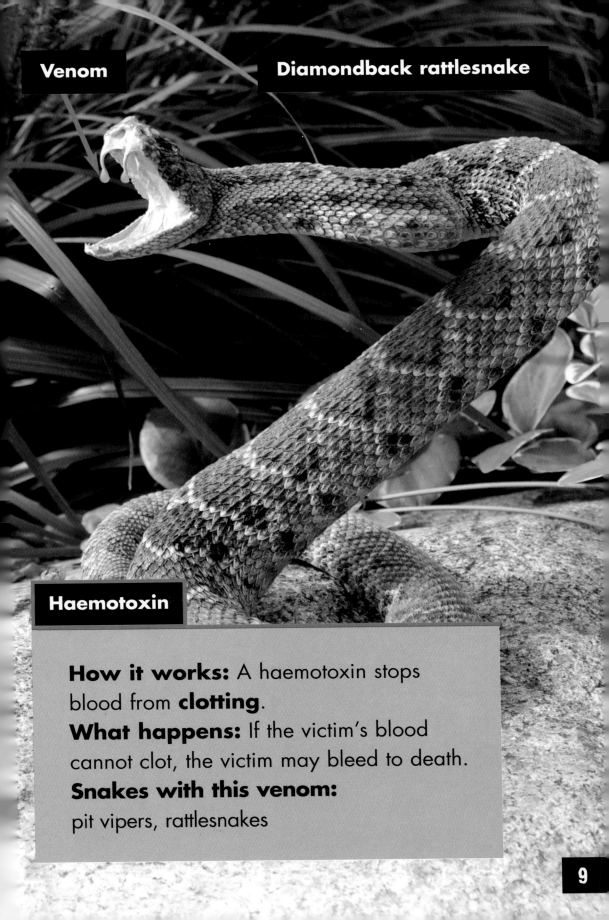

Diamondback rattlesnake

Haemotoxin

How it works: A haemotoxin stops blood from **clotting**.

What happens: If the victim's blood cannot clot, the victim may bleed to death.

Snakes with this venom:
pit vipers, rattlesnakes

TOP KILLERS

The snakes that kill the
most people are the
- Krait (Asia)
- Indian cobra (Asia)
- Black mamba (Africa)
- Puff adder (Africa)

The krait's venom is
the most powerful of the
snakes listed above.

Krait

Kraits are active at night
and they rest in the day.

The most **venomous** snake in the world is the inland taipan. It comes from Australia.

The venom in a single bite could kill 100 people!

Inland taipan

Here, animal expert Steve Irwin holds an inland taipan.

Irwin studied and cared for wild animals at his zoo in Australia. He often worked with dangerous animals, such as snakes and crocodiles.

KING COBRA

When there is a threat, a king cobra will rise up to attack. It makes a hissing sound to warn predators to stay away!

The king cobra is the longest venomous snake in the world. It can grow to over 16 feet (4.8 meters) long.

This is Khum Chaibuddee. In 2006, he set a world record for snake kissing. He kissed 19 king cobras!

In 1999, a Malaysian zookeeper called Mahaguru Sani also set a record. He spent 35 days locked in a room with 250 cobras.

Just one bite from a cobra and the men might have been killed!

BLACK MAMBA

Half of the people bitten by black mambas die.
Even baby mambas have deadly bites!

Mambas normally stay hidden from people.
However, in 2006 there was a heatwave in
South Africa. Baby mambas need heat to survive
while in their eggs. Because it was so hot, more
baby mambas hatched from their eggs than normal.

Hundreds of baby mambas invaded the city of
Durban. They were all looking for a place to live.

The city's snake catchers were kept busy catching
the baby mambas. Thankfully, no one was bitten!

Black mambas are one of the fastest snakes in the world. They can slither faster than most people can run.

DEADLY SQUEEZE

Pythons and constrictors squeeze their prey to death.

These snakes attack by first biting their prey to keep the animals from escaping. Next, they wrap their huge bodies tightly around their prey.

Crocodile

Every time the prey breathes
out, the snake tightens its grip.

The prey **suffocates** to death.

Rock python

SWALLOW HARD

Snakes do not chew their food. They swallow it whole!

First, the snake kills its prey using its venom or squeezing its victim to death.

Mouse

Corn snake

Lower jaw

Next, the snake swallows its prey's head.

A snake's lower jaw is not attached to its upper jaw. This means it can open its mouth very wide.

Then the snake slithers its own body over its meal until everything is inside.

Sometimes, the snake's prey is not dead.
Some snakes do not kill their prey before eating it.

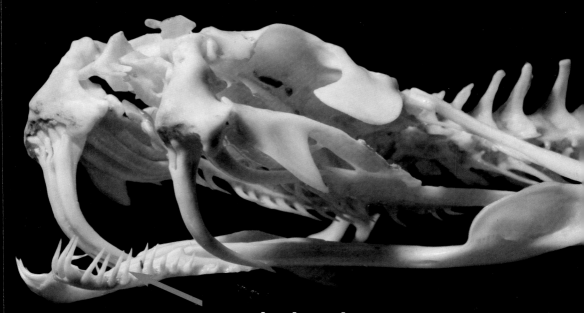

Hooked teeth

Then the snake uses its hooked teeth to hold the struggling prey as it is...

...swallowed alive!

WARNING!

A snake's venom is its main way of catching prey and **defending** itself. So, it does not want to waste it.

Most venomous snakes give a warning before they attack.

Rattlesnake

Rattle

If a rattlesnake is cornered, it will shake the rattle on its tail to frighten the predator off. The rattle is made of dead skin. It grows longer as the snake gets older.

Venomous coral snakes have bright warning stripes on their bodies. The colorful stripes warn other animals to stay away. But some non-venomous snakes also have bright stripes.

A coral snake has red stripes touching yellow stripes.

Coral snake

A kingsnake is non-venomous. Its red stripes touch black stripes.

Kingsnake

Remember this old rhyme:
Red touch yellow,
kill a fellow.
Red touch black,
venom lack.

SURVIVE A SNAKE BITE

When a person is bitten by
a snake he or she should:

- Stay calm and not panic.
  Non-venomous snakes bite, too.
  Even dangerous snakes do not
  always use their venom.

- Keep still. Moving will pump
  the venom around the body.

- Let the bite bleed. Then wash
  and bandage it.

- Remember what the snake looks
  like. He or she will then be able
  to describe it to a doctor.

Get to a hospital quickly!

SNAKE BITE CURES

Snake bites are treated with medicines called **antivenins**

Antivenins are actually made from snake venom!

Indian cobra

The man in this photo is trying to catch an Indian cobra. The man makes a living catching snakes. He catches them so their venom can be collected.

Venom

The venom is then injected into a large animal, such as a horse. The horse's blood makes chemicals to fight the venom. The venom does not hurt the horse.

Samples of the horse's blood are then used to make the antivenin.

SNAKES AND PEOPLE

Snakes do not deliberately attack people.
They usually avoid people whenever possible.

Snakes only bite people if they are
cornered or believe they are in danger.

Sometimes, snakes bite if a person
disturbs them or steps on them.

A snake that is injured might also bite
if it believes a person is a threat to it.

If you are in an area where snakes live, follow these rules to avoid snake bites:

- Avoid areas where snakes may be hiding, such as under rocks and logs.

- Wear long pants and hiking boots when walking through tall grass.

- If you see a snake, leave it alone!

SOS – SAVE OUR SNAKES!

Many **species** of snake are **endangered**. They need help!

People often kill venomous snakes because they are afraid of them. Snakes lose their **habitats** when people clear land to build homes or grow **crops**.

Zoo visitors hold a python.

There is some good news. Zoos give snakes a safe place to live. They also teach visitors about the snakes.

Many zoos are **breeding** endangered snakes. Sometimes zoo-bred snakes can go back to the wild.

The Australian woma python is very endangered.

Woma python

In September 2007, nine zoo-bred womas were put back into the wild in a safe nature reserve.

There are fewer than 250 Aruba rattlesnakes left.

Aruba rattlesnake

Zoos around the world are taking part in about 35 Aruba rattlesnake breeding programs.

EED-TO-KNOW WORDS

antivenin Stops the effects of snake poison

breeding Putting male and female animals together so they mate and have young

captivity Living in a cage or enclosure, such as in a zoo, on a farm, or as a pet

clotting When liquid blood becomes jelly-like and no longer flows

crops Plants grown for food

defend To protect

endangered At risk of dying out so there are no more of that animal species left

fang A long, sharp tooth. Snake fangs are hollow so venom can be pumped through them

habitat The place where an animal lives. Snakes live in many different habitats, from forests to deserts

nerves Fibers that carry messages between the brain, spinal cord, and other parts of the body

prey An animal that is hunted by another animal as food

predator A living thing that hunts and kills other living things for food

species A group of animals that look similar and can breed with each other

suffocate When an animal or person dies because they can not breathe

venom Poisonous saliva

venomous A snake that produces and uses venom to kill prey and to defend itself

victim A person or animal who is hurt or killed

SNAKES AS PETS

Would you like a pet snake? Think it through carefully...

- Many snakes can live for over 20 years. Are you prepared to care for your snake for that many years?

- Keeping a python might seem like fun, but it could grow to over 10 feet (3 meters) long! Do you have enough room?

- Always choose a snake born in **captivity**. Wild snakes should not be captured and kept as pets.

- Get some expert advice: http://animal.discovery.com/guides/reptiles/snakes/main.html

Some people keep corn snakes as pets. They grow up to 5 feet (1.5 meters) long.

SNAKES ONLINE

Do you want to learn more about snakes? Visit these websites:
www.kidsplanet.org/factsheets/snakes.html
www.kidzone.ws/lw/snakes/facts.htm
http://pelotes.jea.com/vensnake.htm
http://www.nationalgeographic.com/kingcobra/index-n.html

Publisher's note to educators and parents:
Our editors have carefully reviewed these websites to ensure that they are suitable for children. Many websites change frequently, however, and we cannot guarantee that a site's future contents will continue to meet our high standards of quality and educational value. Be advised that children should be closely supervised whenever they access the Internet.